HOW TO DRAW YOUR OWN GRAPHIC NOVEL

PENCILLING, INKING AND COLOURING YOUR GRAPHIC NOVEL

FRANK LEE

W
FRANKLIN WATTS
LONDON•SYDNEY

First published in 2012 by Franklin Watts

Franklin Watts
338 Euston Road
London NW1 3BH

Franklin Watts Australia
Level 17/207 Kent Street, Sydney, NSW 2000

Produced by Arcturus Publishing Limited,
26/27 Bickels Yard, 151–153 Bermondsey Street, London SE1 3HA

Text and illustrations: Frank Lee with Jim Hansen
Editors: Joe Harris and Kate Overy
Design: Andrew Easton
Cover design: Andrew Easton

A CIP catalogue record for this book is available from the British Library.

Dewey Decimal Classification Number 741.5'1

ISBN: 978 1 4451 1031 8

Printed in China

Franklin Watts is a division of Hachette Children's Books, an Hachette UK company.
www.hachette.co.uk

SL002071EN
Supplier 03, Date 0112, Print Run 1421

CONTENTS

DRAWING TOOLS

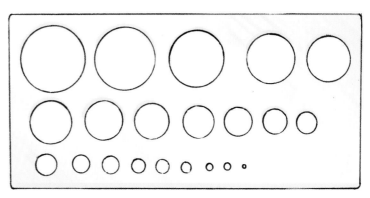

CIRCLE TEMPLATE

This is very useful for drawing small circles.

LAYOUT PAPER

Most professional illustrators use cheaper paper for basic layouts and practice sketches .before they get around to the more serious task of producing a masterpiece on more costly paper. It's a good idea to buy some plain paper from a stationery shop for all your practice sketches. Go for the least expensive kind.

DRAWING PAPER

This is a heavy-duty, high-quality paper, ideal for your final version. You don't have to buy the most expensive brand. Most decent art or craft shops stock their own brand or a student brand and, unless you're thinking of turning professional, these will be fine.

WATERCOLOUR PAPER

This paper is made from 100 per cent cotton and is much higher quality than wood-based papers. Most art shops stock a large range of weights and sizes. Paper that is 300 gsm (140 lb) should be fine.

These are available in a few shapes and sizes and are useful for drawing curves.

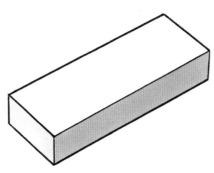

ERASER

There are three main types of eraser: rubber, plastic and putty. Try all three to see which kind you prefer.

PENCILS

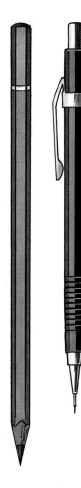

It's best not to cut corners on quality here. Get a good range of graphite (lead) pencils ranging from soft (B) to hard (2H).

Hard lead lasts longer and leaves less graphite on the paper. Soft lead leaves more lead on the paper and wears down more quickly. Every artist has their personal preference, but H pencils are a good medium range to start out with until you find your favourite.

Spend some time drawing with each weight of pencil and get used to their different qualities. Another good product to try is the mechanical pencil. These are available in a range of lead thicknesses, 0.5 mm being a good medium range. These pencils are very good for fine detail work.

PENS

There is a large range of good-quality pens on the market these days and all will do a decent job of inking. It's important to experiment with different pens to determine which you are most comfortable using.

You may find that you end up using a combination of pens to produce your finished artwork. Remember to use a pen that has waterproof ink if you want to colour your illustration with a watercolour or ink wash. It's a good idea to use one of these anyway. There's nothing worse than having your nicely inked drawing ruined by an accidental drop of water!

BRUSHES

Some artists like to use a fine brush for inking linework. This takes a bit more practice and patience to master, but the results can be very satisfying. If you want to try your hand at brushwork, you will definitely need to get some good-quality sable brushes.

MARKERS

These are very versatile pens and, with practice, can give pleasing results.

INKS

With the dawn of computers and digital illustration, materials such as inks have become a bit obscure, so you may have to look harder for these. Most good art and craft shops should stock them, though.

PENCILLING SKILLS

The key to creating great graphic-novel art is to start with simple shapes and very gradually build up detail. Let's start by looking at shapes such as cylinders, cubes and spheres. If you learn how to give three-dimensional form to simple shapes (like the ones below), you will have unlocked the real secret to drawing lifelike figures.

CYLINDERS:

PYRAMIDS:

CUBOIDS:

CUBES:

SPHEROIDS:

SPHERES:

BUILDING A BODY

To create a human figure, you should start with a stick figure, then build on it using simple shapes. To achieve other poses, you just need to reposition these simple shapes. Once you have mastered this step-by-step technique, you'll have the skills you need to draw realistic figures with ease.

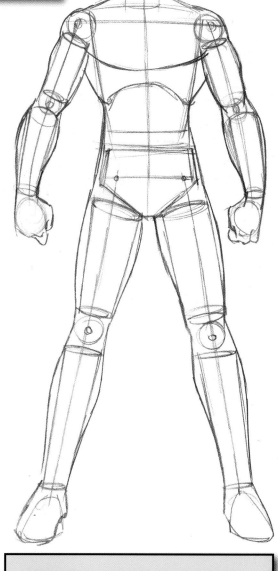

STEP 1

Start by drawing a simple stick figure as your frame. The figure should have shoulders and hips.

STEP 2

Now build your body by adding basic shapes to the stick figure.

STEP 3

Draw around the shapes to produce your figure outline. Once you have established your character's body shape, you can add details.

DRAWING HEADS

The human head can be mapped out using a rectangular grid (see right). This example is based on a standard-sized head, but you can alter these proportions when creating characters with different looks, such as monsters or supernatural beings.

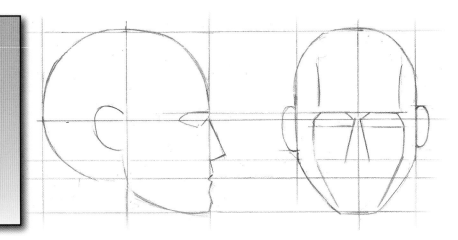

GETTING STARTED

First divide the rectangle into smaller shapes, as shown here. Note that the forehead makes up half the height of the head. Position the eyes on the centre line. The nose should extend downwards from the centre line. The ears should be on the same level as the nose.

Once you have learned these basic steps, try drawing the head from other angles and adding in details.

FLESHING OUT YOUR PENCILS

Once you are happy with the basic pose and attitude of your character, you can start to add more detail.

CLEANING UP

Draw an outline around your basic shapes. Then remove the shapes so you're left with a clean outline. Now you can add detail. Develop your character's clothing, his hair and the tone of his muscle. Think about his facial expression. Sometimes it helps to use a mirror, or ask a friend to pose for you.

SHADOWS

Pencil in areas of light and shade to add depth to your drawing. This will look even more effective once it's inked.

PROPORTION AND PERSPECTIVE

SIZE MATTERS!

It's important that your characters stay the same size from one picture to the next. Artists often measure the height of a character by the number of human heads it takes to make up the character's height.

MALE CHARACTERS

In real life, the average man is about 6 and a half heads tall. However, in comic books, the hero usually stands at about 8 to 8 and a half heads tall.

REGULAR HERO
8 heads tall

WARRIOR
8.5 heads tall

SUPERHEROINE
7.5 heads tall

FEMALE CHARACTERS

Superheroines are generally one head shorter than superheroes. The superheroine below (third from left) is 7 and a half heads tall. The teenage girl standing next to her (second right) is 6 and a quarter heads tall. This makes her taller than a real-life man, but she's still tiny by comic-book standards.

MONSTROUS CHARACTERS

Our final character, the giant on the far right, defies the standard rules that apply to figure drawing. His apelike frame is 9 and a half normal heads tall. However, his head is twice the size of the warrior's! When you create your own characters, don't be afraid to break the rules.

TEENAGE GIRL
Just over 6 heads tall

GIANT
9.5 heads tall

PERSPECTIVE

Now you need to create a world for your characters to inhabit. To make your scenery realistic and believable, a basic knowledge of perspective is necessary.

VANISHING POINT AND HORIZON LINE

Look at the diagram of a train track, below (Fig. 1). Notice how the rails get closer together the further they go into the distance. The point where the lines join is called the vanishing point. The horizontal line in the distance is called the horizon line. The horizon line is the viewer's eye level.

If we continue these lines, they will eventually meet (Fig. 3). The point at which they meet determines the horizon line. This is called a one-point perspective because the lines meet at a single point (Fig. 4).

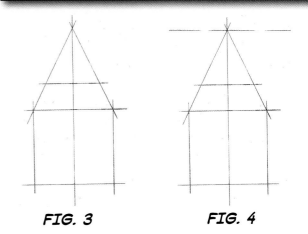

FIG. 3   *FIG. 4*

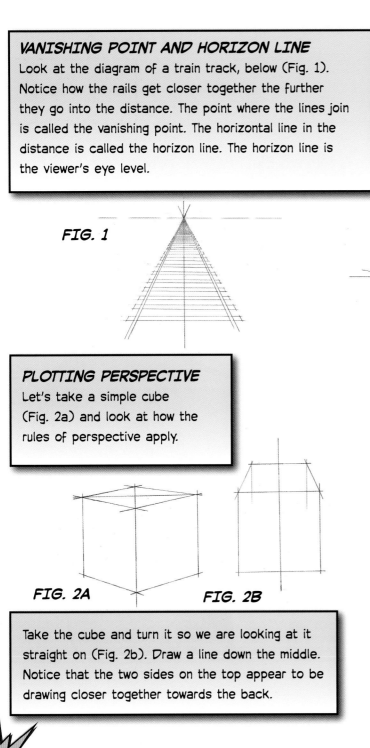

FIG. 1

FIG. 5

PLOTTING PERSPECTIVE

Let's take a simple cube (Fig. 2a) and look at how the rules of perspective apply.

When we turn the cube so we are looking directly at one of the corners, we get a two-point perspective (Fig. 5). This means there are two vanishing points.

FIG. 2A   *FIG. 2B*

FIG. 6

Take the cube and turn it so we are looking at it straight on (Fig. 2b). Draw a line down the middle. Notice that the two sides on the top appear to be drawing closer together towards the back.

Here is the cube from above (Fig. 6). If we follow the converging lines to their ultimate meeting point, we again get a two-point perspective.

USING PERSPECTIVE IN YOUR COMIC ART

Here are some examples of how to apply the rules of perspective to comic-book panels. Even though it's tricky, it's important to try to get the perspective right. To make the scenes in your comic book look as realistic as possible, all the elements in the foreground, background and centre of your page must be positioned correctly. When you have multiple vanishing points, attach another sheet of paper to your drawing so that you can continue the perspective lines off the page to get them just right.

Another example of a two-point perspective.

This scene has been drawn using a one-point perspective.

This example has a two-point perspective.

INKING AND COLOURING

EXAMPLE 1: THE JADE DRAGON

A clean, crisp line style has been used to ink this character, but you may wish to experiment with different styles and textures of your own. Colour has been applied in layers for a rich finish.

There are a number of ways to ink a pencil drawing. Some artists prefer to use a brush and a pot of black Indian ink. We recommend that you use waterproof Indian ink to ink your pencil drawings, so that when you apply colour on top, your ink will not raise or smudge. If you decide to use a brush, a no. 3 sable brush can be used to achieve a variety of line thicknesses.

There are also lots of good inking pens available, with a range of nib thicknesses, including superfine, fine and brush. The brush nib pens are very good as they produce a wide range of line thicknesses, too (see below).

STEP 1

Finish your pencil drawing, marking out any areas of shading to go over in solid, black ink.

STEP 2

Keeping a steady hand, carefully ink over your pencil artwork. Try to make the lines as crisp and precise as you can. The solid areas of black ink will show through after you have applied colour.

STEP 3

Start colouring by applying a dark green base to the clothing.

STEP 4

Now apply a medium skin tone. Don't choose a shade that's too dark, as later we'll layer darker tones on top of this colour to add shading.

STEP 5

Use a lighter shade of green in the central panels of fabric to break up the areas of dark green. A colour called cadmium yellow has been applied to the trim of the suit and the forearm guards.

STEP 6
Finally, shape and tone are added to the skin by using darker, warmer skin tones. The folds in the suit are accentuated by using darker greens with a black or blue hue. A mid-range cool grey has been used for the straps and soles of the boots.

EXAMPLE 2: THE ANNIHILATOR

This character is finished using a variety of different line thicknesses and layers of colour. These techniques give the monster a three-dimensional appearance.

STEP 1
Once you're happy with your pencil drawing, it's time to start inking!

STEP 2
Lots of different line thicknesses are used in this example. In some areas the ink is applied fairly loosely, but in others it is clean and precise. Solid black is used for the mouth area and to define the monster's chest and shoulder muscles.

STEP 3
A light blue followed by a layer of lavender grey is used to create the base colour of the suit.

STEP 4

Cadmium yellow is used as the base tone for the metallic parts of the suit. A cool grey is used for the boots, straps and tubes. Darker shades of grey are layered on to the boots to finish. The toecap is left in the lighter shade.

STEP 5

Sandy shades and orange browns are used to add depth to the metallic areas. Darker shades of grey are layered over the suit to add tonal shading and muscle definition.

STEP 6
White highlights are added to his suit and armour and the darker areas of shading are accentuated. The final touch is his glowing red eyes! This guy is ready for action.

PENCILLING, INKING AND COLOURING A PAGE

THE NEXT LEVEL
Now that you've learned how to ink and colour your character drawings, how about tackling a full page of comic-book art? It's really not that difficult and the same principles apply.

Here we have a page of comic book art in pencil. The solid areas of shading are marked in at the pencil stage, so it's just a case of inking faithfully over the pencil lines.

This artwork would work equally well with even more shading. This would create a stronger contrast between the light and dark areas, but it would leave less room for colour.

As you follow the step–by–step sequence, you'll see how the areas of ink and colour work together in the panels, just as they do when you're colouring an individual figure.

FIG. 1

FIG. 2

INKING STYLES FOR PANELS

Some artists like to ink the panel outlines freehand, without the aid of a ruler. This creates a nice contrast between the panel edge and the clean, crisp lines within the panel (Fig. 1). You can also use a loose line style inside the panel for a slightly sketchier finish (Fig. 2).

INKED PAGE

So here it is – our fully inked comic-book page. When you're creating your own graphic novel, you could choose to keep things simple and leave your artwork in black and white. However the addition of colour will really bring your comic-book pages to life.

We have kept the line style clean and precise throughout. Very little shading has been added so that we have plenty of space left in which to apply colour.

The solid areas of black create dramatic blocks of dark shading. We will also use layers of colour to determine areas of light and shade in the final version.

We used markers to colour the page above, but a similar effect could be achieved using watercolours or liquid inks. Plan your colour palette before you start to apply any colour, and keep it simple!

When colouring your artwork, choose colours that help show what time of day it is. This story is set at night and the light source is the moon. To achieve a moonlit effect, use light blue as your base colour on all panels.

In panel 1 we establish that the light source is the moon. On top of the light blue, layers of olive green and cool grey are applied to colour the trees.

The girl's skin tone and hair are coloured brightly, making her the focal point.

Cool grey is used to add shading to her skin, hair and dress.

Pale blue, olive and grey are also used for panels 2, 3 and 4.

In the final panel we have allowed moonlit areas of pale blue to show through on the trees and grass. This keeps the tone of the light consistent. The glowing eyes in the forest are left white.

LIGHTING AN IMAGE

In the past, the colour in comic strips was fairly basic and simple. The cost of production and the limited technology meant that only flat colours could realistically be used. But nowadays comic-book colouring is increasingly sophisticated. The style of colouring that you choose will affect the overall feel of your graphic novel.

FLAT COLOURS

Some artists prefer to work with large areas of flat colour. This creates a more stylized effect, because it looks less like the real world.

LIGHT AND SHADE

This rich colouring moulds the image. The character looks sculpted and, with light and shade added, she is almost three-dimensional.

COLOUR AND ATMOSPHERE

Colouring can also create a strong sense of time, place and mood. Think to yourself: where is the character? What emotion do you want readers to feel?

WARM COLOURS

This image has a golden tone that feels warm and positive.

COLD COLOURS

These cold blue tones create a sinister, night-time mood.

GLOSSARY

fleshing out The addition of details to a drawing, such as folds in clothes, facial features and shadows.

freehand Drawing a picture without the help of a device such as a ruler or a French curve.

highlights Lighter areas in an artwork, which suggest that light is shining on that area and which add depth to the whole image.

layout A sketch that shows where items, such as figures and words, will be positioned on each page.

panel One of several, usually rectangular, frames in which illustrated scenes appear in a comic book.

perspective A way of drawing items so that they look correctly sized and shaped in relation to each other and in relation to the point from which they are being viewed.

proportions The size of the parts of an object in relation to other parts, such as the size of a head compared to the size of the body in a figure drawing.

stick figure A simple drawing of a figure using sticks and circles.

three-dimensional Having height, width and depth. Comic artists often try to make flat pictures look as if they are three-dimensional (3-D).

tone A shade of a colour, such as light blue or dark green.

FURTHER READING

The Captivating, Creative, Unusual History of Comic Books by Jennifer M Besel
    (Velocity Business, 2010)

How to Draw the Darkest, Baddest Graphic Novels by Asavari Sing (Capstone
    Press, 2011)

Kids Draw: Big Book of Everything Manga by Christopher Hart (Watson–Guptill,
    2009)

Write Your Own Graphic Novel by Natalie M Rosinsky (Capstone Press, 2009)

You Can Do a Graphic Novel by Barbara Slate (Alpha Books, 2010)

WEBSITES

Drawing Comics and Anime
www.drawcomics.net

Drawing Comics: Video Tutorials
http://www.ehow.com/video_4754254_draw-comics.html

Drawing Manga: Video Tutorials
http://www.youtube.com/user/markcrilley

INDEX